Rainforest

Sarah Levete

Published 2011 by
A&C Black Publishers Ltd.
36 Soho Square, London, W1D 3QY

www.acblack.com

ISBN HB 978-1-4081-3366-8
PB 978-1-4081-3367-5

Text copyright © 2010 Sarah Levete

This book is produced using paper that is made from wood grown in managed, sustainable forests. It is natural, renewable and recyclable. The logging and manufacturing processes conform to the environmental regulations of the country of origin.

Produced for A&C Black by Calcium. www.calciumcreative.co.uk

Printed and bound in China by C&C Offset Printing Co.

All the internet addresses given in this book were correct at the time of going to press. The author and publishers regret any inconvenience caused if addresses have changed or sites have ceased to exist, but can accept no responsibility for any such changes.

Acknowledgements

The publishers would like to thank the following for their kind permission to reproduce their photographs:

Cover: Shutterstock
Pages: Dreamstime: Shariff Che' Lah 9, Ryszard Laskowski 14, Michael Lynch 13, Xiaobin Qiu 3, 12, Steveheap 7, Swisshippo 4, Lawrence Wee 19; Shutterstock: 7877074640 1, 11, Nina B 20, Todd Boland 21, Steve Bower 16, Joseph Calev 6, Hannamariah 18, Giancarlo Liguori 5, Dr. Morley Read 8, 15, Chai Kian Shin 17, Worldswildlifewonders 10.

Contents

Rainforests

Many animals, plants, and trees are found in **rainforests**. Some are beautiful, some are strange.

Amazing animals

Bright green lizards called geckos live in the rainforest. They have sticky **toe pads** to help them hold on tight as they climb up tall rainforest trees.

Toe pad

Hot and wet

Tropical rainforests are found in hot parts of the world. It rains most days in these forests.

The gecko gobbles up insects.

Tall Trees

Animals live in every part of the rainforest, from the forest floor to the top of the trees. Only a few, such as birds, can reach the tallest trees.

High and low

The scarlet macaw swoops up to the sunny treetops to build its nest. Larger animals make homes on the forest floor.

The macaw has beautiful, bright feathers.

Wobble, wobble!

People who study rainforest animals use wobbly rope bridges to cross the treetops.

Rope bridge

Bug Alert

The rainforest buzzes with insects. Some, like ants, help clean up the rainforest by eating dead leaves and animals.

Tiny killers!

Hundreds of **army ants** march together, stinging anything in their way. These tiny crawlers can sting a snake to death.

Army ants have a deadly sting.

Important insects

Dragonflies spread **seeds** when they land on flowers. The seeds grow into new plants.

Tree House

Monkeys live high up in the trees. They make a lot of noise, calling out to each other as they leap about.

Hang on!

Spider monkeys have strong tails to help them swing between branches. They grab tasty fruit with their long arms as they swing from tree to tree.

Tail

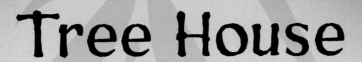

Monkeys are fantastic climbers.

Upside down!
Sloths sleep hanging upside down from the rainforest trees!

In the Air

During the day, colourful birds glide through the treetops and peck at fruit. At night, bats flap and swoop about in the dark.

Beaky eater

The toucan makes its home in small holes in rainforest trees. Its tough beak is perfect for breaking open hard nuts.

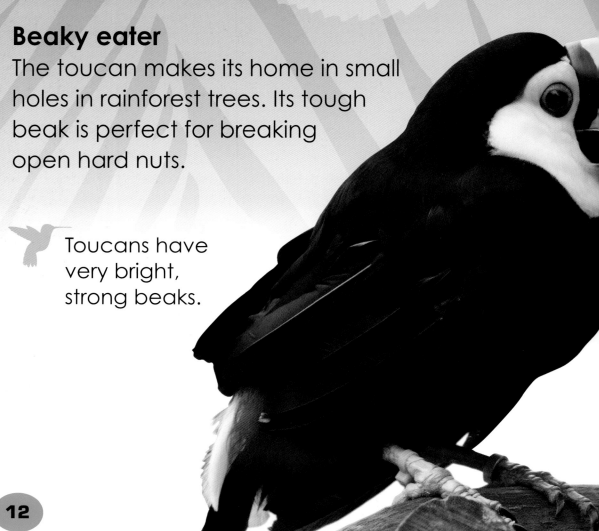

Toucans have very bright, strong beaks.

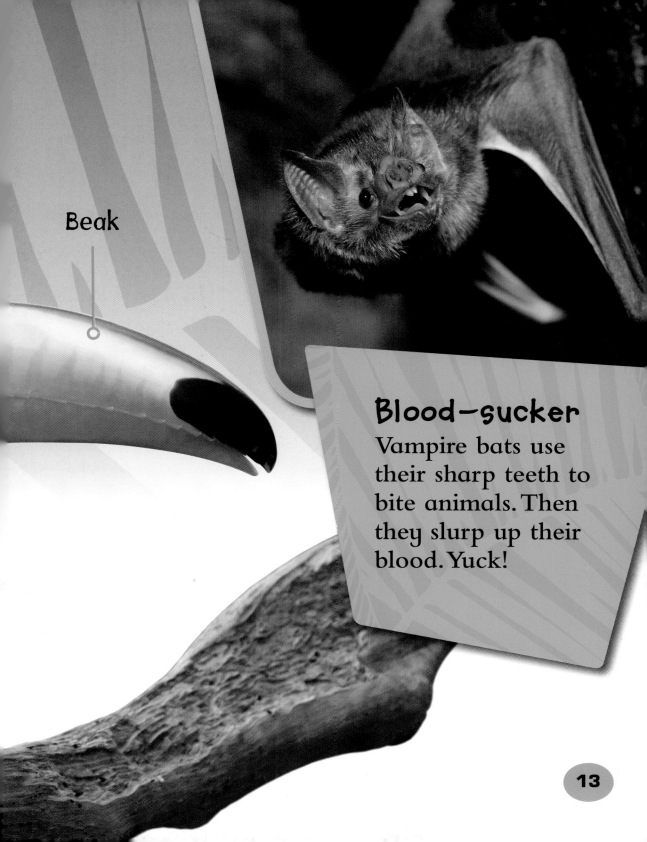

Beak

Blood-sucker

Vampire bats use their sharp teeth to bite animals. Then they slurp up their blood. Yuck!

Splash!

Long, winding rivers flow through rainforests. These are home to many animals such as capybaras.

Water home

Capybaras graze on grass that grows at the river's edge. If cabybaras are in danger, they just swim into the river using their **webbed** feet.

Capybaras eat their own poo!

Snap!

Crocodiles rest in
river water until
they spot a tasty
animal to snap
up and swallow.

Plant World

Plants and flowers grow everywhere in the rainforest. Insects land on them, and frogs even live in them.

Home, sweet home

Frogs live inside brightly coloured plants called bromeliads. The plant's big leaves fill up with rainwater to make a perfect swimming pool for rainforest tree frogs.

Tree frog

Hungry plant

The pitcher plant traps small animals and insects before eating them up!

Tree frogs lay eggs in plants.

Danger!

Rainforest animals work hard to stay alive and find food. Some are fierce **hunters**, others use colour to stay safe.

Deadly

The boa constrictor snake slides along the rainforest floor and trees, hunting for food. When it finds a victim to eat, it squeezes it to death before swallowing it whole!

I'm warning you

The bright markings on its wings warn enemies that this butterfly is **poisonous**.

Marking

This snake is as long as two grown ups.

Our Home

Local people have lived in the rainforests for many years. They live in houses they have built.

Living here safely

Rainforest people know which plants and animals can be harmful and which are safe to eat. They also look after the rainforest.

Feather

Rainforest people make clothes from plants and feathers.

Pretty good

This pretty pink plant is used to make **medicine**.

Glossary

army ants type of ant that has a poisonous sting

hunters animals that look for other animals to eat

medicine something that makes people feel better if they are ill

poisonous harmful if eaten or touched

rainforests thick forests where it rains most days

seeds parts of a plant that can grow into other new plants

sloths furry animals with very long claws that live in rainforest trees

toe pads sticky pads on an animal's feet that stick to the surface it is climbing on

tropical parts of the world where the weather is hot and wet all year round

webbed covered by a flap of skin to help animals swim

Further Reading

Websites

Discover more about rainforests, the animals and plants that live there, and how much rain falls on the forests at: **www.enchantedlearning.com/subjects/rainforest**

Find out lots more about rainforests and the animals that live there at: **www.globio.org/glossopedia/article.aspx?art_id=6**

Books

Rainforest (Eye Wonder) by Elinor Greenwood, Dorling Kindersley (2001).

Rainforest (Usborne Beginners) by Lucy Beckett-Bowman, Usborne (2008).

Rainforests (Totally Weird) by Kate Graham, Two-Can (1998).

Index